A Competitive Pound for a Stronger Economy

GW00535609

A Competitive Pound for a Stronger Economy

John Mills

Civitas: Institute for the Study of Civil Society
London

First Published October 2013

© Civitas 2013
55 Tufton Street
London SW1P 3QL

email: books@civitas.org.uk

ISBN 978-1-906837-56-3

Independence: Civitas: Institute for the Study of Civil
Society is a registered educational charity (No. 1085494)
and a company limited by guarantee (No. 04023541).
Civitas is financed from a variety of private sources
to avoid over-reliance on any single or small group
of donors.

All publications are independently refereed. All the
Institute's publications seek to further its objective of
promoting the advancement of learning. The views
expressed are those of the authors, not of
the Institute.

Typeset by Kevin Dodd
Printed in Great Britain by
Berforts Group Ltd
Stevenage SG1 2BH

Contents

	Page
Author	vi
1. Is Austerity the Only Way?	1
2. Cutting Public Expenditure	6
3. Increasing Purchasing Power	11
4. The Exchange Rate	20
5. Objections	24
6. Conclusion	37
Notes	39

Author

John Mills is an entrepreneur and economist. He graduated in Philosophy, Politics and Economics from Merton College, Oxford, in 1961. He is currently chairman of John Mills Limited, a highly successful import-export and distribution company.

He has been Secretary of the Labour Euro-Safeguards Campaign since 1975 and the Labour Economic Policy Group since 1985. He has also been a committee member of the Economic Research Council since 1997 and is now Vice-Chairman. He is also Chairman of The People's Pledge campaign for a referendum on Britain's EU membership, and Co-Chairman of Business for Britain.

He is the author of *Growth and Welfare: A New Policy for Britain* (Martin Robertson and Barnes and Noble 1972); *Monetarism or Prosperity?* (with Bryan Gould and Shaun Stewart Macmillan 1982); *Tackling Britain's False Economy* (Macmillan 1997); *Europe's Economic Dilemma* (Macmillan 1998); *America's Soluble Problems* (Macmillan 1999); *Managing the World Economy* (Palgrave Macmillan 2000); *A Critical History of Economics* (Palgrave Macmillan 2002 and Beijing Commercial Press 2006); and *Exchange Rate Alignments* (Palgrave Macmillan 2012).

He is also the author of previous Civitas pamphlets *A Price that Matters* (2012) and *An Exchange Rate Target* (2013).

1

Is Austerity the Only Way?

In 1976 Prime Minister James Callaghan told the Labour Party conference: 'We used to think that you could spend your way out of a recession, and increase employment by cutting taxes and boosting government spending. I tell you in all candour that that option no longer exists.' What he said may have been good politics, reflecting the pessimistic mood in Britain as the country, racked by inflation, falling output and civic discontent, turned to the IMF for succour. It was, however, at least in part, doubtful economics. Recessions happen because there is insufficient demand to keep everyone occupied productively. The only solution is more demand and not less. Increases in demand, however, require major contributions from both the private as well as the public sector to be sustainable. James Callaghan was therefore surely right in saying that the public sector could not provide the solution on its own.

Economists and policy makers, however, have a long history of looking the other way and ignoring the need for more demand to combat recessions. The Austrian School, typified by writers such as Friedrich von Hayek, always maintained that the slumps which followed booms should be allowed to take their course as what Andrew Mellon, Herbert Hoover's Treasury Secretary at the onset of the Great Depression, described as the 'rottenness' flowing from over-exuberant expansion is purged by deflation. Indeed, Mr Mellon's formula was 'Liquidate labor, liquidate stocks, liquidate the farmers, liquidate real estate', even claiming that the panic which accompanied the market collapsing was no bad thing.[1] Those opposed to the state performing a larger role than they believe is strictly necessary, while not necessarily going all the way with Andrew Mellon, have nevertheless usually been reluctant to encourage governments to stimulate the economy. Their preference has been to rely more heavily on the private sector for recovery than may always be warranted by experience. When times are hard, most people understandably have little sympathy with bailing out individuals and companies which overstretched themselves by gambling against the odds that the good times would last forever. Allied to these sentiments are fears that borrowing money to stimulate demand might increase inflation and incur more debt than can be afforded.

These sentiments, however, leave those economies where they are most prevalent in dire condition. Much of Europe, including the UK, is already suffering from levels of GDP lower than when the current financial crisis started, with little prospect of improvement in the near future. We may well be into at least a decade of no growth which would have been an almost unthinkable prospect during the boom period prior to 2008. Unfortunately, anaemic growth since 2008 and falling living standards have ground down optimism that we ought to do better than this – indeed much better if we were bold enough. Even the Labour leadership is now talking about accepting most of the economic policy framework established by the Coalition government. Almost everyone seems resigned to there being no alternative to years of low or non-existent growth for the foreseeable future. At the moment, what little increase in GDP there is in the UK barely keeps up with population growth. No wonder that living standards are stagnant, when they are not falling.

As a result of this consensus that slow growth and high unemployment are inevitable, and that cut-backs and austerity are the only way ahead, we are in great danger that our economic performance is going to remain dismally poor for the foreseeable future. Without radical rethinking, the UK and much of the West more generally may sink into the same sort of economic torpor which has gripped Japan for almost all of the last two decades, although there are signs that very recent policy changes may alter the picture there for the better. After the stellar economic performance which Japan achieved during the 1960s and 1970s, followed by lower but still respectable growth rates in the 1970s and 1980s, who during any of those years would have predicted that the Japanese economy would slump down to a growth rate averaging no more than 1.7 per cent for all the years between 1992 and 2011? Allowing for population growth, the position has been even worse. GDP per head only rose by an average of 0.8 per cent per annum over the whole of this twenty year period.[2] The Eurozone faces a similar prospect. Eurozone GDP in 2013 is still two per cent lower than it was in 2008.[3] Allowing for population growth averaging 0.4 per cent[4] per annum over this period, GDP per head has fallen by just over three per cent. This is a dismally bad result with little prospect of recovery to 2008 levels for several years to come, if then. In the UK the position is even worse. In mid-2013, GDP per head was just over six per cent lower than it had been in the last quarter of 2007.[5]

The performance of the US economy, however, while still mired in excessive debt, is nevertheless better than in most of Europe. US GDP increased by 8.5 per cent between the second quarter of 2009 and the first quarter of 2013.[6] With population growth averaging 0.9 per cent per annum, GDP per head in 2013 was 3.7 per cent ahead of the 2008 figure.[7] US policy over this period was much more growth-oriented than in Europe, partly because the remit of the Federal Reserve is much broader than that of the European Central Bank or the Bank of England. The Fed is obliged to take into account key factors such as unemployment rates as well as inflation, thus producing a combination of fiscal and monetary policy which has been much more conducive to recovery than has been the case in Europe. The US experience shows that the very poor economic results that have been achieved in the UK and on the continent of Europe are not necessarily inevitable. The key issue then is how to make them better and whether there are ways of making even the US experience look lacklustre.

Is there a way to reignite substantial rates of growth in the West? This pamphlet argues that there is, although perhaps not to the growth rates currently being attained by much of the developing world. With western living standards as high as they are, it seems only reasonable that those with lower GDP per head should be allowed to catch up. As advanced

4

economies move to having an ever higher proportion of their GDP created by services rather than manufacturing, their growth rates tend to slow in any event compared to economies where manufacturing predominates to a greater extent. This occurs because productivity growth is much easier to secure in manufacturing than in services. The problem faced by many western economies, however, is not whether they should grow at four per cent or eight per cent per annum but how to achieve any increase in output and living standards at all. There may be a case for keeping annual increases in GDP modest compared to those in the less developed world. This is an altogether different proposition to facing the prospect of stagnation for years ahead.

2

Cutting Public Expenditure

One of the most immediate impacts of the financial crisis has been a very large increase in government deficits. In the UK the deficit rose from £36.4bn in 2007 to a peak of £156.3bn in 2009, when the government was borrowing one in every five pounds it spent.[8] Similar figures were to be seen in the USA and across much of the Eurozone. Clearly borrowing on this scale is unsustainable, especially if combined with economic output which is stagnating at best or falling at worst. The policy very widely adopted to deal with this pressing problem was to reduce public expenditure. If government expenditure is higher than its receipts from taxation, fees and charges, then it seems only logical that the way back to viability is to cut government spending.

Unfortunately, however, what seems obvious is not necessarily correct. There is a familiar fallacy of composition in thinking that what might make sense to one part of the economy, taken in isolation, makes sense for the economy as a whole. To understand why this should be the case, consider why these much larger deficits appeared in the first place. There were two main reasons. One was the natural result of falling tax receipts and rising welfare expenditure as economies contracted. The other was the necessity of shoring up demand during a recessionary period to avoid the fall in economic output across Western economies being even greater than would otherwise have been the case.

The key to understanding why this is so is to look at the way government deficits are financed. The money has to come from other sectors of the economy – of which there are three. There is the corporate sector, there are households and there is the rest of the world. The Office for National Statistics publishes all the relevant borrowing and lending data for the UK, updated every quarter. The figures for all the years since 2000 are set out in Table 1 below.

Table 1: UK Borrowing and Lending, 2000-2013

All figures in £ 000,000

	Total Govt. Borrowing	All Corporations	Household	Rest of the World	Totals
2000	13,986	−30,012	−10,295	26,321	0
2001	7,665	−25,262	−4,927	22,525	1
2002	−20,143	14,708	−16,045	21,479	−1
2003	−40,829	44,428	−21,571	17,973	1
2004	−41,733	57,978	−39,834	23,588	−1
2005	−40,313	61,784	−45,897	24,425	−1
2006	−35,001	51,465	−54,587	38,123	0
2007	−38,372	75,153	−66,374	29,593	0
2008	−70,698	99,557	−40,031	11,172	0
2009	−152,053	110,173	27,779	14,100	−1
2010	−147,013	95,986	17,447	33,580	0
2011	−120,140	96,787	14,363	17,006	8,016
2012	−99,853	28,133	24,674	53,974	6,928
2013 Q1	−23,689	12,788	−6,488	13,898	−3,491
Annualised	−94,756	51,152	−25,952	55,592	−13,964

The key feature of the figures in this table is that they have to sum to zero, since all lending has to be matched pound for pound by exactly the same amount of borrowing. This is the case in the table for all the years between 2000 and 2010. There are discrepancies between 2011 and 2013 only because the ONS has not yet finally reconciled all the figures for these years. When this has been done, the net figure for these years will also be zero.

The figures in the table show clearly what happened in the UK as the crisis hit the economy from 2007 onwards. Until 2012, corporations continued to retain profits, lending them to the rest of the economy at a rate of around £100bn a year, rather than investing to increase production. The dip in 2012 was due to special one-off factors, as explained further below.

Households, on the other hand, moved between 2007 and 2009 from being net borrowers to net lenders, with a swing of nearly £100bn. It was very largely this movement which was reflected in the huge increase in the government deficit. The household sector became much more cautious about the future, borrowing much less than it had done previously while paying down existing debt. To avoid the economy then collapsing for lack of demand, and to make up for falling revenue caused by diminished tax receipts and increased welfare claims, the government had no practical alternative but to borrow much more heavily to close the gap between its income and expenditure.

The crucial policy issue now is to establish what, in the light of these figures, can be done to bring government borrowing down to a manageable level. Some combination of three things has to occur. Either corporations have to reduce their net lending by investing more, or households have to save less and spend more, or the foreign payments deficit – financed by lending from abroad – has to be reduced. What are the prospects for any of these things happening?

Business net lending fell dramatically in 2012 but appears to be bouncing back in 2013. The ONS attributes the huge fall in 2012 mainly to two easily identifiable special factors – the transfer of the Royal Mail pension scheme assets and profit on quantitative easing lending being credited to the government – and a third, more volatile component, which was a large drop in net property income.[9] It appears, however, to be unlikely on the latest trends that net lending by the corporate sector is going to be much less than £50bn to £60bn per annum in future, unless there is a substantial increase in business optimism. Yet, if the economy has little prospect of significant growth in the reasonably near term, it seems unlikely that sufficient business confidence will materialise for there to be the surge in investment needed to reduce the corporate lending figure below this level.

The first quarter of 2013 showed a sharp change in consumer behaviour with a big swing to net borrowing, much of it, no doubt, associated with increased activity in the mortgage market. If this could be maintained, it would certainly help to reduce the government deficit, but whether this will happen remains to be seen as living standards are squeezed by prices rising faster than incomes. Taking this into account, it seems more likely that the net borrowing figure for households in 2013 will be closer to zero than £26bn. This then leaves net borrowing from abroad, which has grown significantly in 2012 and 2013 as the foreign payments balance has deteriorated.

This ought to be the area where government could do most to rectify the position, but on present trends there is little sign of this happening. Taken together, figures of £60bn for foreign borrowing and £50 to £60bn for corporate borrowing indicate that the government deficit is likely to be between £110bn and £120bn. This view is shared by the Office for Budget Responsibility (OBR).[10]

This analysis sheds a harsh light on the impact of efforts to cut the deficit without taking into account these other drivers of government borrowing. Cutting government expenditure is much more likely to cut GDP than reduce the government deficit. This is because cutting overall demand is likely to depress rather than increase either corporate or household confidence. Nor is it likely to make any significant difference to our foreign trade deficit. The result will then be about the same level of government deficit as before, but with equilibrium between the main borrowing and lending components being established at a lower level of national output. This would be due to a familiar combination of falling government revenue and rising welfare expenditure.

This dismal prospect is strongly reflected in the experience of both the Coalition government in the UK and the weaker economies in the Eurozone. It may well be the case that government expenditure is uncomfortably high as a percentage of GDP and well in excess of the income available to finance it in all these economies, but the way to tackle this problem is not to cut public expenditure. It is to improve business and consumer confidence and to get the foreign payments deficit under control.

3

Increasing Purchasing Power

If the UK and many other Western economies are currently experiencing a toxic combination of poor growth and rising public indebtedness, to overcome these problems we clearly need much more sustainable purchasing power to raise both consumer and corporate confidence. We also need to ensure that this increase in purchasing power does not leak abroad as a result of increased import penetration. James Callaghan was right in saying that the state on its own could not provide the cure to deflation. Deficit financing is not enough. A major contribution also has to be made by the private sector through increased investment, rising consumer confidence and better net external trade performance.

The standard reaction to this challenge is to rely on a wide variety of supply side initiatives. These include policies for improving education and training, investing in infrastructure, easing expanding companies' access to finance, providing tax breaks for private investment, reforming the planning system to make new developments easier, and many other ways of making the economy operate more efficiently. There is no doubt that approaches of this sort have intrinsic merit and that, when there is sufficient demand, they would all be part of the mix needed to ensure that the economy performed better. The problem, however, is that policies of this sort do little or nothing to solve the problem of lack of demand. In the absence of more purchasing power, all these policies to improve efficiency and productivity will tend not to increase output but merely to redistribute existing output in a depressing zero sum game. If total output stays the same, as a matter of simple logic, increased output per head in one part of the economy has to be matched by falling productivity somewhere else.

How then, can increased demand be achieved in a way which will enable economies such as ours to grow in a sustainable way? This is the crucial policy issue to which almost the whole of the western world needs to find a solution. The analysis set out above may provide a way ahead which is required not only to get the West's economies expanding again but also to avoid many of them becoming insolvent as both their governments' and their economies' indebtedness continue to expand much faster than their capacity to service and repay it. Taking the UK as an example, if by 2015 total government debt is approaching 100 per cent of GDP and is still rising at the rate of just below eight per cent per annum – as it is at the moment if special factors are ignored – and with the current account deficit continuing to run at four per cent of GDP, with no realistic prospect of either ratios improving, the UK's position will clearly become increasingly unsustainable.

There is a way to resolve the problems we face but it will require a very radical change to the approach adopted for a long time in formulating policy for the British economy. It involves focusing on the lack of competitiveness of the UK economy internationally and using the exchange rate to engineer a transformation in the prospects for the future of our GDP.

Table 2: UK Share of World Exports, 1950-2010

All figures in $000,000

Year	UK	World	%
1950	6,325	59,000	10.7%
1960	10,606	118,800	8.9%
1970	19,428	289,700	6.7%
1980	110,137	1,931,700	5.7%
1990	185,268	3,423,400	5.4%
2000	281,800	6,360,100	4.4%
2010	410,300	15,087,800	2.7%

Source: International Financial Statistics 1989, 2000 and 2012; IMF, Washington DC.

First, we need to recognise just how uncompetitive the UK economy has been for a long period and how uncompetitive it continues to be. Table 2 shows what has happened to our share of world exports over the 60 years between 1950 and 2010, which is as good a measure as any of our declining export competitiveness compared with our competitors. The reason why our share of world trade has gone down so dramatically is not just because other economies have become much more important than they were before. It has happened mainly because our exports have grown so much more slowly than the world average, reflecting the weak performance of the UK economy as a whole. Table 3 shows the huge increase in the exchange rate from which the UK economy has suffered, particularly ever since monetarist ideas became fashionable around 1980, although there is ample evidence that sterling had been much too strong for most of the period since the start of the industrial revolution. It is the over-valuation of sterling which has made our exports so uncompetitive and so stunted our growth rate.

Table 3: Chained Real Effective Exchange Rate Indices, 1975-2011

	IMF 1989 Data	IMF 2000 Data	IMF 2004 Data	IMF 2012 Data	Chained Data
1975	83.6				83.6
1976	76.1				76.1
1977	75.6				75.6
1978	82.0				82.0
1979	97.3				97.3
1980	120.1				120.1
1981	123.3				123.3
1982	114.5				114.5
1983	103.7				103.7
1984	99.8				99.8
1985	100.0	112.0			100.0
1986	92.6	103.5			92.4
1987		104.6			93.6
1988		111.5			99.8
1989		109.0			97.5
1990		110.9			99.2
1991		115.0			102.9
1992		109.8	74.0		98.2
1993		98.6	65.8		88.2
1994		101.2	67.7		90.5
1995		100.0	67.8		89.5
1996		103.1	71.8		94.7
1997		126.7	88.3		116.5
1998			95.6		126.2
1999			96.0		126.7
2000			100.0	123.7	132.0
2001			97.3	128.9	128.4
2002			98.9	123.8	130.5
2003			94.9	111.6	125.2
2004				102.7	115.2
2005				100.0	112.2
2006				99.8	112.0
2007				93.2	104.6
2008				90.9	102.0
2009				97.3	109.2
2010				92.8	104.1
2011				86.3	96.8

Sources: International Financial Statistics Yearbooks 1989, 2000, 2004 and 2012: IMF, Washington DC. Based in all cases on Relative Unit Labour Costs

14

Paying our way in the world depends very heavily on our performance in selling manufactured goods and also being able to produce domestically a reasonable proportion of those that we consume. About two thirds of our exports and three quarters of our imports are manufactures.[11] Although the UK's performance on sales of services abroad and providing for our own domestic requirements for them has been much better than on manufacturers, the volume of internationally traded services is nothing like sufficient to fill the gap on goods. The UK's visible trade deficit is now running at over £100bn a year, or more than six per cent of GDP, only about three quarters of which is covered by our trade surplus on services.[12]

The UK's inability to pay its way in the world has not just caused us to have chronic balance of payments problems. The last time we had a surplus on visible trade was in 1982 and we have not had an overall positive foreign payments balance since 1983.[13] Worse than this has been the impact of our weak payments balance on our ability to run the economy at full throttle for fear that doing so would make the foreign balance position even worse. It has also reduced the effectiveness of policies designed to stimulate demand in the economy because the increased purchasing power is transferred abroad through increased import consumption.

This, combined with lack of confidence in future expansion by both the corporate sector and – more recently – by consumers, has led to the economy growing consistently more slowly than it could and should have done. This is partly why our growth rate has for a long time been much slower than the world average and why unemployment in the UK is so high. Between 1970 and 2011, UK GDP per head increased by an annual average of no more than 1.7 per cent, while in Singapore it was 4.6 per cent, in South Korea it was 6.4 per cent and in China it was 7.9 per cent. The world average was 1.8 per cent.[14]

There is, however, another reason why our growth rate has been so much below that of other countries. Productivity increases are much easier to achieve in manufacturing than they are in services. In the UK, between 1997 and 2012, gross value per head rose in manufacturing by 62 per cent compared to 18 per cent for the economy as a whole, despite the fact that over this period manufacturing as a percentage of UK GDP, fell from 14.5 per cent to 10.7 per cent[15] as a result of unmanageable competition from abroad. Similar figures are to be found in the US where during, for example, the last two decades of the 20th century, productivity in manufacturing rose by 57 per cent compared to 17 per cent for the economy as a whole.[16]

Table 4 models the impact of varying exchange rates on an exporting firm's profit margins. For simplicity's sake, it is assumed that it is a British firm exporting to the USA so that we are only concerned with the sterling/dollar exchange rate. The price of the hypothetical good is $100 per unit. The firm receives dollars from sales of the good which are used to pay for production costs. These fall essentially into two categories. On the one hand there are internationally determined costs such as material inputs and depreciation, which are fixed by world prices, usually charged in dollars. On the other hand

Table 4: The Impact of the Exchange Rate on an Exporting Firm's Profit Margins

Revenue and costs per unit sold:

	£1 = $1	£1 = $0.8	£1 = $1.2
Revenue	$100	$100	$100
Internationally determined costs			
Material inputs	$20	$20	$20
Depreciation	$10	$10	$10
Domestically determined costs	$60*	$48	$72
Total cost per unit	$90	$78	$102
Net profit per unit in dollars	$10	$22	−$2
Net profit per unit in sterling	£10	£27.5	−£1.67

* Sterling domestic cost of each unit is £60.

there are a whole variety of domestically determined costs that are paid in sterling covering the provision of a wide range of activities from taxi journeys to accounting services and from printing stationery to repairs and maintenance. Most of this category is ultimately labour costs but it also includes other types of input costs such as rent and interest charges. These are assumed, excluding a margin for profit, to be £60 per unit. Internationally determined costs are unaffected by the exchange rate as they are paid in dollars. The value of domestically determined costs, however, varies with the sterling/dollar exchange rate as these are paid in pounds. The lower the value of the pound is to the dollar, the fewer dollars does the British exporter need to pay its domestically determined costs and the higher is the profit earned.

Table 5: How Devaluation Allows an Exporting Firm to Gain Market Share

Revenue and costs per unit sold:

	\<A\>	\<B\>	\<C\>
	£1 = $1	£1 = $0.5	£1 = $0.5
Revenue per unit exported	$100	$100	$65
Internationally determined costs			
Material inputs	$20	$20	$20
Capital depreciation	$10	$10	$10
Domestically determined costs	$60*	$30	$30
Total cost per unit	$90	$60	$60
Net profit in dollars	$10	$40	$5
Net profit in sterling	£10	£80	£10

* Sterling domestic cost of each unit is £60.

Exporters in low cost-base countries tend, however, not to use their exchange rate advantage to make large percentage profits on their sales. Instead, they opt to gain market share by increasing the volume of their sales. Table 5 is another simple model which shows how and why they do this. The starting assumptions here are the same as for Table 4. Column A shows the initial position, where £1 = $1 and the exporting firm makes a £10 sterling profit per unit sold. In this example we assume a 50 per cent devaluation in Column B. Material input and depreciation costs stay the same but domestic costs fall by half, increasing sterling profit per unit to £80. Column C shows how the exporting firm could take advantage of the devaluation to lower its sales price per unit to $65, significantly undercutting international competitors, while still making the same sterling profit of £10 per unit that it made prior to the devaluation. This is the sort of strategy that low cost countries have used time and again to gain share of world trade. No wonder that our over-valued currency has caused our share of world trade to decline.

The relative size of the manufacturing sector in a developed and diversified economy is a critical issue which has been barely addressed in the UK. Even as late as 1980, just under a quarter of the UK's GDP came from manufacturing. This ratio has now dropped to little more than 10 per cent. Despite this huge fall, well over half our export earnings still come from visible rather than invisible exports. As we have deindustrialised, so our trade balance has deteriorated. The same process has taken place in many other western countries such as the USA, France, Spain and Italy – although to a significantly lesser degree in Germany. It appears that there is a tipping point at about 15 per cent of GDP. Once manufacturing's share of GDP drops below this percentage it becomes impossible for the countries concerned to pay their way in the world. The resulting foreign payments deficits then make running their economies at anything like full throttle impossible. The result is the stagnation, high unemployment, increasing inequality and declining international significance which is all too characteristic of most western economies, including ours.

4

The Exchange Rate

The UK economy needs lower average export prices to enable our exporters to compete in world markets. To achieve this, we clearly need to stop over-charging the rest of the world for our domestically incurred production costs. The UK needs to set an exchange rate that is sufficiently competitive to help us recover our export capacity and ability to pay our way in the world. This would help us get back to a growth rate of three to four per cent per annum – about the world average – and to get unemployment down to perhaps three per cent. How much would we have to devalue? The depreciation needed depends on how responsive manufactures are to pricing, and there is a wealth of information available on this subject. The latest meta-study to be carried out was published by the IMF in 2010.[17] This showed that the UK – as was the case with all other countries – easily passed the Marshall-Lerner condition, which is that for a devaluation to produce long-term positive effects, the sum of the export and import elasticities (ignoring the negative sign for imports) has to be more than unity. In the UK's case the export elasticity was 1.37 and the import elasticity was 1.68.[18] Incidentally, the higher import elasticity figure shows how important import substitution is. Taking a rather cautious view of these elasticity figures, we need to get sterling down by roughly one third to achieve a three to four per cent growth rate and to get unemployment down to four per cent.

Reducing the exchange rate by about one third

would have a dramatic effect on both our capacity to sell more exports and our propensity to import. Net of any efforts made by foreign suppliers to reduce their margins to hold onto market share, imports would become 50 per cent more expensive than they were before, thus very strongly encouraging home production of goods when previously it was much cheaper to buy in from abroad. For exporters, however, the position would be reversed. Typically for manufacturers, as we have seen, about 20 per cent of their costs are raw materials and 10 per cent is depreciation of fixed assets, for both of which there are world prices. All the remaining 70 per cent (including a provision for profit) are domestically incurred charges which would fall with the exchange rate. This means that foreign buyers could be charged 21 per cent (30 per cent of 70 per cent) less than before while the manufacturing exporter still makes the same percentage return on sales.

Some manufacturing operations are located where they are because they are protected by government contracts, intellectual property rights, longstanding expertise and supply chains or by exceptionally good management. Very large areas of manufacturing, however, do not fall into any of these categories. It will just go to where the cost base is charged out at the most favourable rate, which is where the exchange rate is most competitive. In this context, it is interesting to see companies such as Caldeira UK and Hayter, marketing respectively cushions and mowing machines, moving significant parts of their operations back to the UK following the 2007/2009 devaluation.[19] This shows that there is no insuperable obstacle to increasing our manufacturing capacity and paying our way in the world again, provided that exporting manufactures abroad and producing them for the domestic market is made to be more profitable and importing such goods correspondingly less so. It also explains why such a big exchange rate change as a reduction by one third is required. If we need to get the UK proportion of GDP derived from manufacturing back to about 15 per cent, some very powerful price signals are going to be required to make this happen.

It is now possible to see how relatively easy it would be to get the borrowing and lending figures discussed earlier back to where they need to be. A major objective behind a more competitive rate for sterling would be to eliminate the foreign payment deficit and the need to borrow from abroad. Increasing exports and producing domestically more of the goods we currently import would greatly improve growth and investment prospects in the economy. This would in turn encourage the corporate sector to deploy a much larger proportion of its net profit into investment instead of lending it to the rest of the economy. Consumers are also likely to feel much more confident and therefore to become more willing to borrow. A possible outcome in these circumstances might be no net borrowing or lending by any of the major components of the economy, in which case the government deficit would fall to zero. Even if this benign state was not reached, a movement in such a direction would help to put the economy on a much more sustainable footing than at present. For example, a smaller devaluation might create a foreign payments deficit of, say, £30bn. If this was combined with net lending by the corporate and household sectors of, say, £10bn each, the government deficit would be a manageable £50bn per annum.

5

Objections

If there is a solution to our economic problems along the lines set out above, why do we not adopt it? Part of the reason is that discussion of the exchange rate has simply slipped off the public agenda. For example, the exchange rate was not mentioned once during the parliamentary debate on the Autumn Statement in December 2012. The only mention of it in the accompanying 97-page Treasury document was buried in a table on page 87 which merely tells us that the Office of Budget Responsibility projects no change in the value of sterling *vis-à-vis* the euro during the next five years. The exchange rate is one of the most powerful economic levers available to government. Adopting the right rate can be highly beneficial, while getting it wrong can cause huge damage. Yet for a long time there has been little discussion of the importance of the exchange rate in either the press or the academic world. This urgently needs to change.

There are, however, also frequently rehearsed arguments for not even considering an active exchange rate policy which strongly buttress the view that nothing should be done to promote one. What are these objections and how valid are they? Taking them in turn:

Devaluations always lead to more inflation, which means that any price advantage initially gained is soon lost.

There is a very widely held view, strongly buttressed by monetarist theorising, which makes it something of an article of faith that increased import prices caused by a lower exchange rate must automatically trigger an inflationary spiral which will soon wash away any initial gain in competitiveness. Those who hold these views, however, have clearly not studied the wealth of statistics available which show that no such thing usually happens in the real world. There are dozens of cases in recent economic history when devaluations have happened and in not a single one is there any evidence that the devaluing country has failed to gain a significant, at least medium-term, competitive advantage. Of course there are countries such as Italy, which for many decades after World War II had a higher rate of inflation than its main competitors and gained therefore only a temporary advantage from its repeated devaluations. Italy's condition would, however, have been much worse without periodically re-establishing its competitive position. The key point is that, with almost all devaluations, there is little evidence of any increase in inflation other than what would have been expected anyway. Furthermore, in many cases the rate of inflation actually fell – as it did in the UK when we came out of the Exchange Rate Mechanism (ERM) in 1992 and the exchange rate fell by 19 per cent. The GDP deflator, a common measure of inflation, was 6.7 per cent in 1991, four per cent in 1992, 2.8 per cent in 1993 and 1.5 per cent in 1994.[20] A devaluation can produce disinflationary impacts in several ways.

First, one of the immediate impacts of a devaluation is to make all domestic production more competitive in both home and export markets. This is bound to lead to increased output, although there will inevitably be time lags before the benefits of it come through. Eventually this will reduce average costs because greater utilisation of existing capacity would allow overhead charges to be spread across a higher quantity of output.

Second, some of the policies associated with bringing the value of the currency down directly affect both production costs and the cost of living generally. One of the most important of these is the rate of interest at which most borrowing is done. This almost invariably comes down with the exchange rate. Indeed, lowering the cost of borrowing is part of the mixture of policy changes needed to get parities reduced. High real rates of interest are a heavy and expensive burden on most firms. They are also an important component of the retail price index, particularly in countries where a large proportion of personal outgoings are on variable rate loans, such as mortgage payments.

Third, as a lower exchange rate expands output it becomes possible to lower consumption taxes, such as VAT, or national insurance. Companies usually pass on the value of these taxes to the consumer in the form of higher prices. These taxes are significant components of the value of the retail and consumer price indices, the most common measures of inflation. Reducing them will therefore lead to lower consumer prices and inflation.

Fourth, rising productivity, which flows from increased output, not only has the immediate effect of reducing costs. It also makes it possible to meet wage claims of any given size with less impact on selling costs. Nor is this just a factor which applies for a short period until those responsible for formulating wage claims adjust to a new situation and then increase their claims. The international evidence strongly suggests that economies with rapidly expanding output have a better wage negotiation climate generally, and thus achieve increases in remuneration more realistically attuned to whatever productivity increases are actually being secured.

Fifth, one of the major objectives of devaluing is to switch demand from overseas sources to home production. While the price of imports is bound to rise to some extent, there is strong evidence that the increase in costs from exchange rate changes are seldom passed on in full. Foreign suppliers are inclined to absorb some of the costs themselves, calculating that they may make up what they lose on the margin they earn by holding on to market share. Furthermore, if demand is switched from imported goods and services to home production, this purchasing power will not be affected – at least not directly and in full – by the increase in import prices. It will benefit in cost terms from the fact that domestic output is now relatively cheaper than purchases from abroad.

Devaluations cause living standards to fall.

Although it seems as though it must be true that, if sterling is depreciated, living standards in the UK must go down because the UK is selling its services for cheaper prices in world terms, this is not what actually happens. The reason for this apparent paradox is that UK living standards are measured in pounds and not in world currencies such as dollars. Although a big sterling devaluation would obviously reduce UK GDP measured in dollars, it would have no immediate effect on UK national income measured in the currency with which UK residents actually do nearly all their shopping, which is sterling. In this vitally important respect, Harold Wilson was right when he told the country after the 1967 devaluation that: 'It does not mean that the pound here in Britain, in your pocket or purse or in you bank, has been devalued.'[21]

The fact that this is the case shows up clearly in the statistics produced by organisations such as the IMF. Far from economically declining, nearly all devaluing countries subsequently grow faster than they otherwise would have and their export performance improves. If population size stays constant but GDP grows, then as a matter of mathematical logic, GDP per head must increase.

Some qualifications must, however, be made. If a devaluing country's economy is at nearly full stretch when its currency depreciates, and subsequently a higher proportion of its output is exported, there may have to be some shift in income distribution towards exports and away from domestic consumption. Also if, as a result of better economic prospects, investment goes up, this will have to be reflected somewhere in more savings. In practice, however, these effects tend to be easily swamped by rising GDP. This is why, in case after case, the effect of devaluations is to increase living standards. Over the period of the 1992 UK devaluation, for example, the real wage rose by 0.2 per cent in 1990, 1.9 per cent in 1991 and by a remarkable 7.6 per cent in 1992, before falling back to 1.6 per cent in 1993 and 1.2 per cent in 1994.

Exchange rates are fixed by market forces and governments or central banks cannot change them.

Any country's exchange rate is determined by the interplay of a variety of different factors, of which the trade balance may not be the most significant. Interest rate differentials attract capital inflows to countries with higher interest rates, pushing up the exchange rate. Capital inflows caused by foreign direct investment can also be a major factor. Undoubtedly, a major reason why sterling was so strong in the 2000s was that there was a huge volume of UK asset sales to foreign interests over this period. Between 2000 and 2010, net inward portfolio investment totalled £615bn,[22] dwarfing the UK's cumulative £287bn foreign payments deficit over the same period.[23] The $2 valuation of the pound during much of the 2000s was far too high for many of the UK's manufacturing exporters to cope with, which is why there was the fall in manufacturing as a percentage of UK GDP over this period from just under 15 per cent to not much more than 10 per cent.[24] The drop from $2 to $1.60-$1.50 by the middle of 2013 was still therefore nothing like large enough to make most UK produced manufactures competitive in world markets.

The exchange rate can therefore be very substantially affected by interest rate and direct investment policies which are both under government control. In addition, there are many other policies which governments can use to shift exchange rates if they are determined to do so, as we have seen recently in the case of both Switzerland and Japan. The Swiss central bank was determined to stop the Swiss franc strengthening as money seeking a safe haven poured into the country recently. It succeeded in stopping the franc rising above 1.20 to the euro despite all the market pressure there was to make the franc stronger.[25] Japan reduced the value of the yen against the dollar by over a third between the end of September 2012 and the end of April 2012.[26] How could the UK get sterling to depreciate? Demand could be expanded, partly by flooding the country with liquidity, to produce a temporary worsening in the foreign current account balances, as Japan has done. The Bank of England could sell sterling. It, or the government, could announce a target exchange rate, as did the Swiss, making it clear that the chosen rate would be defended with sufficient vigour to make speculating against it not worthwhile. Once it became obvious that the government was determined to see the exchange rate at a different level, the market would respond accordingly provided that the government's strategy was co-ordinated well enough to make it clearly credible. The enormous fluctuations there have been in exchange rates among all countries since 1971, when the Bretton Woods system broke up, show only too clearly that exchange rates, far from being immutably fixed by market forces, are capable of very wide fluctuations and are very largely influenced by policies under government control.

Any one country devaluing would very probably trigger off other devaluations elsewhere, leading to a zero sum war of competitive devaluations.

Clearly, it is impossible for every country to improve its economic performance by depreciating its currency.

Every devaluation has to be matched by an equal and opposite revaluation somewhere else. However, some economies have a much stronger case for a more competitive currency than others. There are a number of tests which are clearly applicable. Any country, especially one which is developed and diversified and which has consistently lost share of world trade, is evidently a strong candidate. Table 2 (page 13) clearly shows that this has been the case for the UK economy. So are countries which have high levels of unemployment, slow growth and serious problems in balancing their foreign payments positions. The real villains of the piece are not, in fact, countries which have big deficits. It is those that consistently accumulate large surpluses – such as Japan, Germany, Switzerland, China, Taiwan and the major oil producing countries – thereby accentuating the problems of all the economies with weaker foreign payment positions. These countries are as responsible as anyone for the world's current economic instability.

Nor is it remotely in the world's interest to have large numbers of its major economies in the sort of financial difficulties currently exhibited by much of the western world. The unmanageably large trade and borrowing imbalances which are currently accumulating make no sense for anyone. It would be far better if manufacturing were distributed evenly enough round the world to enable all economies to pay their way without having to pursue deflationary policies to contain otherwise dangerously large deficits. Excluding countries with very large proportions of their economies devoted to the production of raw materials, the average proportion of GDP devoted to manufacturing across the world is about 16 per cent.[27] It would be reasonable to allow relatively undeveloped countries to have a rather higher share than this, to enable them to grow more quickly than the world average and to catch up with richer countries. It makes no sense, however, to have economies such as ours which cannot pay their way in the world or grow significantly because manufacturing as a proportion of our GDP is now barely above ten per cent.

There is thus an extremely strong case to be advanced to our international partners that it is in everyone's interest for highly uncompetitive countries such as the UK to be allowed to set their currencies at more realistic levels. If this cannot be done without international co-operation, however, there would be nothing to stop a determined British government from getting sterling down to a competitive level unilaterally and still with not much likelihood of retaliation. It should not be the intention of the British government to run a balance of payments surplus, thus destabilising other countries. Nor is it in other countries' interest to see both the UK economy and its government getting so indebted that it runs the risk of default. Against this background, a devaluation of sterling to the level needed to rebalance our economy, especially as our share of world trade is now so small – it had fallen to 2.7 per cent by 2011[28] – could hardly disrupt the world's economic system significantly. When sterling fell from its peak of $2.11 in 2007 to $1.36 in 2009[29] – a fall of 35 per cent – there was no retaliation. Why should the situation be any different now if there is another similar percentage fall?

The UK has tried devaluations before and they do not work.

Excluding the fall in the value of sterling between 2007 and 2009, there have been three major devaluations of sterling since the end of World War II. In 1949 the pound was devalued by 31 per cent against the dollar from $4.03 to $2.80. In 1967, it fell a further 14 per cent from $2.80 to $2.40. Over the next 25 years the rate fluctuated widely, as monetarist policies were implemented. These were aimed primarily at reducing inflation with scant attention paid to what these policies might do to the competitiveness of the British economy. There was a particularly low point of a $1.03 valuation in March 1985, rising to $1.70 by December 1989. The period when sterling was in the ERM, locked to the Deutsche mark at DM 2.95, ended with the third major devaluation when the UK fell out of the ERM in September 1992. The pound fell by 34 per cent against the DM between September 1992 and February 1993,[30] and in real effective terms against all currencies by about 15 per cent.[31]

Each of these devaluations led to higher growth and employment than would have been the case had they not occurred. All the major downward movements in the UK exchange rate, however, were too little and too late, mainly because none of them took anything like sufficient account of the higher rates of inflation on average in the UK compared to our international competitors. A telling example is to compare the Swiss with the UK experience. Between 1970 and 2010, the average rate of inflation in Switzerland was 1.6 per cent. In the UK it was 5.6 per cent. Over this 40 year period, the price level rose 88 per cent in Switzerland and by 780 per cent in the UK.[32]

Nor has a strong penchant for an over-valued currency been a recent phenomenon in the UK. After the Napoleonic Wars, as a result of the deliberations of the Select Committee on the High Price of Gold Bullion, the UK went back to the pre-war parity between sterling and gold, unlike almost all the other combatants. The resultant high value for sterling did not cause the UK too much of a problem during the early stages of industrialisation, as at that stage we had no serious competitors, but when other countries started to copy what we were doing we started to lose ground rapidly. In the meantime, the early nineteenth-century controversy between the Banking and Currency Schools was won by the hard-money currency camp, leading to the 1844 Banking Act which in turn established the framework – again with sterling too strong – for the Gold Standard which lasted until World War I. Between 1850 and 1914, the UK saw its share of world trade fall steadily while it grew more slowly than our competitors. When World War I came, inflation in the UK was much higher than in the USA, but this did not stop the Cunliffe Committee recommending in 1918 that the pre-war parity between sterling and the dollar be re-established. This goal was finally achieved in 1925, causing the whole of the 1920s to be marred by unemployment, low investment and a feeble rate of growth as the UK's competitive position deteriorated.

In 1931, the UK devalued by just over 30 per cent against the dollar and by 24 per cent against all other major currencies[33] with dramatically favourable results. In the five years to 1937, manufacturing output rose by 48 per cent. Between 1932 and 1937 the UK economy grew cumulatively at 4.6 per cent per annum[34] – the fastest rate of growth we have ever achieved over any five-year period. By the end of the 1930s, however, mainly as a result of devaluations elsewhere which the UK authorities did nothing to counteract, all the competitive advantage we had secured earlier on in the decade had been lost. The UK economy was managed in many respects much better during World War II than during World War I, but by the end of hostilities it was heavily overburdened with war debts – particularly the sterling balances owed to Commonwealth countries, an overhang of imperial ambitions that could no longer be afforded, and a currency much too strong to be competitive. The result – yet again – was a falling share of world trade, slower growth and higher inflation than elsewhere.

As inflation mounted in the 1970s, the Keynesian consensus broke up and monetarist ideas took their place. Inflation fell from its 24.2 per cent year-on-year peak in 1975 but at huge further cost to our competitiveness as the figures in Table 3 show.[35] Nor was the counter-inflationary strategy particularly successful. Prices were actually rising slightly faster when Margaret Thatcher left office in 1990 than they were when she became Prime Minister in 1979.[36] This was followed by the disastrous period of over-valuation while we were in the Exchange Rate Mechanism. There was some recovery after we left the ERM in 1992, but our growth rate was still relatively low compared with many other parts of the world and it was clearly too dependent on borrowing and asset inflation. The problem with trying to keep inflation down to as low as two per cent is that the policies needed to achieve this target are almost identical to those needed to keep the exchange rate far too high. After compounding this problem in the 2000s by selling a huge portfolio of UK assets to overseas buyers, we are still left with an overvalued pound as Table 3 shows.

Indeed it is because sterling was so over-valued during the 2000s that we have been blinded into thinking that a $1 to $1.50 valuation must be competitive because this is much less than $2. It is not, as our share of world trade and our balance of payments show all too clearly. But it is also not true that there was no response to the reduction in sterling's value. In volume terms, our exports of manufactured goods grew by 16 per cent between 2009 and 2011 and by 28 per cent by value. The problem was that sterling was still far too strong for import substitution to be a major factor. As a result, from a higher base, manufactured imports rose over the same period by 14 per cent measured by volume and 19 per cent by value.[37] Even so, these figures show a significant improvement and were certainly much better than would have been the position if sterling had remained at $2 to £1.

6

Conclusion

The UK is at a crossroads. Both our government and our nation's debts are rising at a substantially faster rate than our GDP and our capacity to service, let alone repay them. The growth that we are likely to achieve over the next few years, if present policies are maintained, will be much too low to stop the UK drifting further and further towards insolvency and maybe even default. While this happens, unemployment will rise, inequality will increase and our status internationally will decline.

Perhaps this assessment is too gloomy. In its March 2013 Economic and Fiscal Outlook report, the OBR projects the UK economy achieving a growth rate of 2.8 per cent by 2017, as the government deficit falls from its current 7.7 per cent to about three per cent and our foreign payments deficit more than halves.[38] These projections, however, are based on the exchange rate staying exactly where it is now for the next five years.[39] The OBR therefore appears to believe that both the UK's growth rate and net trade performance will improve very substantially with no reduction in the value of sterling. This looks like a heroic assumption – unfortunately in line with the OBR's record since its establishment of being over-optimistic about the recovery which they expect the UK economy to achieve.

Instead, we need to ensure that the performance improvements the OBR hopes for are made to happen, using a much more competitive exchange rate as the vehicle for getting this done. Then we could look forward to a faster growing economy, falling un-employment, falling regional and social-economic inequalities and to holding up the UK's position in the world. For far too long, the key significance of getting the exchange rate right has been ignored. Now, maybe at the eleventh hour but still not too late, we can make the changes that the country so badly needs.

Notes

1   Paul Krugman, 'The Conscience of a Liberal', *The New York Times,* November 2007, available at: http://krugman.blogs.nytimes.com/2007/11/07/purging-the-rottenness/?_r=0 [Accessed 09/08/2013].

2   See GDP volume Measures in: *International financial Statistics Yearbook 2000,* IMF: Washington DC, p164-165. *International financial Statistics Yearbook 2004,* IMF: Washington DC, p113. *International financial Statistics Yearbook 2012,* IMF: Washington DC, p76.

3   Data obtained from: Eurostat Table 'Real GDP growth rate – volume', ref: tec00115, available at: http://epp.eurostat.ec.europa.eu/tgm/table.do?tab=table&init=1&plugin=1&language=en&pcode=tec00115 [Accessed 09/08/2013].

4   See Country Tables in: *International financial Statistics Yearbook 2012,* IMF: Washington DC.

5   Data obtained from: Eurostat Table 'GDP per capita in PPS', ref: tec00114, available at: http://epp.eurostat.ec.europa.eu/tgm/table.do?tab=table&init=1&plugin=1&language=en&pcode=tec00114 [Accessed 09/08/2013].

6   Tyler Holden, Whitehouse.gov blog post, 31st July 2013, available at: http://www.whitehouse.gov/blog/2013/07/31 [Accessed 09/08/2013].

7   *International financial Statistics Yearbook 2012,* IMF: Washington DC, p790.

8   *The Guardian,* 'Deficit, national debt and government borrowing – how has it changed since 1946?', available at: http://www.guardian.co.uk/news/datablog/2010/oct/18/deficit-debt-government-borrowing-data# [Accessed 09/08/2013].

9   IBID.

10   OBR Economic and Fiscal Outlook, March 2013, p6, available at: http://cdn.budgetresponsibility.independent.gov.uk/March-2013-EFO-44734674673453.pdf [Accessed 09/08/2013].

11 ONS Quarterly National Accounts statistics 2013 Q1, Table H1, available at:
http://www.ons.gov.uk/ons/dcp171778_314093.pdf
[Accessed 09/08/2013].

12 2012 ONS Pink Book, p40, Table 1.2, available at:
http://www.ons.gov.uk/ons/rel/bop/united-kingdom-balance-of-payments/2012/index.html
[Accessed 09/08/2013].

13 2012 ONS Pink Book, p37, Table 1.1.

14 Data compiled from the following sources:
International financial Statistics Yearbook 2000, p164-165.
International financial Statistics Yearbook 2012, p76.
The population figures are obtained from country by country tables. World are figures from the UN.

15 ONS unpublished tables showing SIC aggregates.

16 Ibid.

17 IMF Working Paper WP/10/180, available at:
http://www.imf.org/external/pubs/ft/wp/2010/wp10180.pdf
[Accessed 09/08/2013].

18 See average, long run elasticity figures over 2001-2004 period on Pages 15 & 21 of the IMF paper.

19 David Merlin Jones, *The Boomerang Economy*, London: Civitas 2012, p8-9 and p65-66.

20 *International Financial Statistics Yearbook 2000*, p169.

21 BBC 'Wilson defends "pound in our pocket"', available at:
http://news.bbc.co.uk/onthisday/hi/dates/stories/november/19/newsid_3208000/3208396.stm
[Accessed 09/08/2013].

22 2011 ONS Pink Book, p66, Table 7.1, Row HHZD, available at:
http://www.ons.gov.uk/ons/rel/bop/united-kingdom-balance-of-payments/2011/index.html
[Accessed 09/08/2013].

23 2012 ONS Pink Book, p29, Table 1.1.

24 ONS Tables showing estimates of Gross Value Added by SIC.

25 Bloomberg, 'Swiss Ministers Seek More Depreciation of "Strong" Franc', 28th Jan 2013, available at:
http://www.bloomberg.com/news/2013-01-27/swiss-ministers-seek-more-depreciation-of-strong-franc.html
[Accessed 09/08/2013].

26 CNBC,'Currency Devaluation—How to Get Away With It', 9th May 2013, available at:
http://www.cnbc.com/id/100725315
[Accessed 09/08/2013].

27   McKinsey & Company Report, 'Manufacturing the future: The next era of global growth and innovation', November 2012, available at: http://www.mckinsey.com/insights/manufacturing/the_future _of_manufacturing [Accessed 09/08/2013].

28   *International Financial Statistics Yearbook 2012*, p67.

29   See 'Historical Rates' section of *fxtop.com*, available at: http://fxtop.com/en/historical-exchange-rates.php?MA=1 [Accessed 09/08/2013].

30   'Oanda' Historical Exchange Rates, available at: http://www.oanda.com/currency/historical-rates/ [Accessed 09/08/2013].

31   *International financial Statistics Yearbook 2000*, p116.

32   Multiple IMF and Swiss data sources were used to compile these figures.

33   Thelma Leisner, *Economic Statistics 1900-1983*, London: *the Economist* 1985, Table UK.15.

34   Ibid, Table UK.2.

35   House of Commons Library Research Paper, 'Inflation: the value of the pound 1750-2011', p14, available at: http://www.parliament.uk/briefing-papers/RP12-31 [Accessed 09/08/2013].

36   Professor Tim Congdon points out that the rate of inflation, measured by the Retail Price Index, was 10.1 per cent when Margaret Thatcher came to power in 1989 and 10.9 per cent when she resigned in 1990. See his article: 'Whatever the folklore, Lady Thatcher did indeed commit a U-turn when it came to anti-inflation policy', IFS School of Finance, available at: http://fw.ifslearning.ac.uk/Archive/2013/june/features/ howitreallyturnedout.aspx [Accessed 09/08/2013].

37   2012 ONS Pink Book, p40-42, Table 2.1 and 2.2.

38   OBR Economic and Fiscal Outlook, March 2013, 'Executive Summary' chapter, p5-16.

39   See 'Euro/Sterling exchange rate' row of 'Table 4.1: Determinants of the fiscal forecast' on p87 of the OBR Report.